THE ART OF
Pedaling

A Manual for the Use of the Piano Pedals

HEINRICH GEBHARD

with an Introduction by
Leonard Bernstein

DOVER PUBLICATIONS, INC.
Mineola, New York

Bibliographical Note

This Dover edition, first published in 2012, is an unabridged republication of
the work originally published by Franco Colombo, Inc., New York, in 1963.

Library of Congress Cataloging-in-Publication Data

Gebhard, Heinrich.
  The art of pedaling : a manual for the use of the piano pedals / Heinrich
Gebhard ; with an introduction by Leonard Bernstein.
    p. cm.
  Includes bibliographical references and index.
  ISBN-13: 978-0-486-48827-1 (alk. paper)
  ISBN-10: 0-486-48827-6 (alk. paper)
  1. Piano—Pedaling. 2. Piano—Instruction and study. 3. Piano—Studies
and exercises. I. Title.

MT227.G4 2012
786.2'1938—dc23

                                                                    2011041202

Manufactured in the United States by Courier Corporation
48827601
www.doverpublications.com

To the Memory of my Master
THEODOR LESCHETIZKY

Contents

Introduction

READING THIS BEAUTIFUL BOOK HAS BEEN IN THE NATURE OF A recaptured experience for me—the tenderly nostalgic re-experiencing of an old set of emotions. So clearly does the essence of the Gebhard personality emerge in his writing that it transported me almost physically back into his gracious studio in Brookline, Massachusetts, absorbing again the gentle urging, the massive charm, the malice-free wit, and the overwhelming love for music (romantic as a young lover is romantic) that stamped each piano lesson I had with him as a major event. We would sit at two fine old Mason and Hamlins, abreast: I would play, he would play: he would leap up, with that light, deer-like energy, and over my shoulder coax my Mason and Hamlin to sigh and sing like his. Anything I did that pleased him was magnified into a miracle by his enthusiasms: my failures were minimized and lovingly corrected. And all was bathed in the glow of wonder, of constant astonishment at the golden streams of Chopin, the subtle might of Beethoven, the fevered imaginings of Schumann, and the cooler images of Debussy. But nothing ever became really cool. Sound, in itself, was passion; the disposition of sound into constellations for the piano was life itself. I never once left that studio on my own two feet: I floated out.

During my last year of study with this Delphic fountain, I came upon, and was infatuated with, the *Variations* by Aaron Copland. A new world of music had opened to me in this work —extreme, prophetic, clangorous, fiercely dissonant, intoxicating. The work was unknown to Heinrich. "Teach it to me," he said, "and then, by Jove, I'll teach it back to you." And that is precisely what happened. Obviously Gebhard's greatness as a teacher resided mainly in his greatness as a student. Not long before his death he wrote me that he was in the midst of "reviewing" the works of Bach and *The Ring of the Nibelungen*. By Jove, that was a great man.

—LEONARD BERNSTEIN

Preface

FINE PIANO PLAYING REQUIRES MANY ESSENTIALS—TONE, TECHNIC, rhythm in all its varieties, phrasing, dynamics—and the use of the pedals, especially the proper use of the damper pedal. Most of these features are well taught by many teachers and well carried out by average players and students. But the teaching of the musical and artistic use of the damper pedal is still in a fragmentary state.

It is strange that, with this fascinating and extensive field fairly begging for recognition, only a few fine musical scholars have written about it. The artistic and tasteful use of the pedal adds immeasurably to the interest and beauty of a performance, and, indeed, is an intrinsic part of interpretation—its neglect is incomprehensible.

This unfortunate situation is aggravated by the numerous editions of classic and romantic piano literature that contain either very few or very inadequate pedal marks. Sometimes the delightfully laconic expression "con pedale" is put at the beginning of a composition, tickling our sense of humor, as we say "easy way out of it!"

It is particularly surprising that the greater portion of Debussy's and Ravel's piano music contains not a single pedal mark. The color and atmosphere of this music depend crucially on the correct use of the damper pedal.

There are some editions that contain excellent and complete pedal marks, such as Edwin Hughes' fine editions of concertos and other works, and Percy Grainger's edition of the Grieg Concerto. Some modern composers have published their piano music with complete pedal marks. Many teachers have thoughtfully taught where to use pedal and where to omit it. And, of course, the great pianistic giants of the concert stage invariably use the pedal with great taste and art.

But, as a whole, the teaching of the use of the damper pedal is in an embryonic state. It is not too much to say that the great piano-playing public uses either too much pedal or too little.

Some sentimental players, especially amateurs, intending to play with feeling, blur measure after measure of a piece. "They let their feet fall asleep on the pedal," Leschetizky used to say. Others, mortally afraid of it, use so little that an *Allegro* of Beethoven sounds like a Czerny Etude. Very, very few have found the happy medium.

It is a common misapprehension that when the damper pedal is not used, the piano is in its natural. state. *Just the opposite is true. The pianoforte is derived from the harp and the dulcimer, and when the damper pedal is depressed and all the strings are free to vibrate, it is in its natural state.* When the "loud" pedal is down any tone struck on the piano *sings;* all its overtones vibrate in sympathy with the note struck. The piano sounds alive. The damper pedal actually should be called the "live" rather than the "loud" pedal. When the damper pedal is up (raised) the tone of the piano is cool, crisp and crystalline; when it is down (depressed) the tone is rich, sonorous and glowing.

Anton Rubinstein called the damper pedal "the soul of the piano." In piano literature we find an immense variety of music, from simple homophony to complex counterpoint, and the vibrating singing quality of tone provided by the damper pedal is not always desired. Accordingly, this pianistic resource should be used with the greatest musical and artistic discrimination. Some compositions should be played with a good deal of pedal, some with a moderate amount, and some with none at all. Also, we must take into account that in the higher register of the piano, from about 𝄞 up, we may hold the pedal through scales and even contrapuntal passages, for they do not blur much there, owing to the thinner quality of the tone. From about 𝄞 down, if there are scales or contrapuntal passages, we must use little pedal, or none at all.

This book is not an exhaustive treatise on the use of the damper pedal. That would be an impossible undertaking—it would take volumes to explore all the musical combinations of sound possible by the use and non-use of the pedal. But the author has classified the most important uses (and non-uses) of the pedal into certain principal categories. Under each of these categories passages are quoted from piano literature, to illustrate specific effects. The musically intelligent student, after reading the text under each heading and playing the passages with the pedaling indicated—listening carefully to the effect produced—should apply that pedaling to other passages which fall into the same musical category.

It is hoped that the book will help the average student develop a more definite feeling and instinct for musical and artistic pedaling.

H.G.

The Damper Pedal

1. TECHNIC OF THE FOOT

Place the ball of the right foot on the damper pedal, the foot in line with the pedal with the heel, like a pivot, solidly on the floor. The up-and-down movement (done with relaxed ankle) must be noiseless. The foot must *press* the pedal, not leave or strike it. When the pedal is down, it must be *completely* down, when it is up, it must be *completely* up. *The ball of the foot must always be in contact with the pedal,* whether it is up or down. This can be felt through the sole of the shoe.

2. PEDAL MARKS

The pedal marks in this book are to be understood thus: The mark ⌞_____⌟ stands under the staff. The note above the beginning of the mark is to be taken ("caught") with the damper pedal. This is done by putting the pedal down *a moment after* the opening note is struck. Almost all opening notes of a phrase should be executed thus. The pedal should be released exactly where the mark ends.

From here on the word "pedal" means the damper pedal.

3. MAKING SINGLE UNCONNECTED NOTES VIBRATE WITH THE PEDAL

BEETHOVEN, *Sonata, Op. 27, No. 1*

MOUSSORGSKY, *Pictures at an Exhibition*

MAKING SINGLE UNCONNECTED CHORDS VIBRATE

BEETHOVEN, *Sonata, Op. 2, No. 2*

BEETHOVEN, *Sonata, Op. 110*

MAKING UNCONNECTED BROKEN CHORDS VIBRATE

MOZART, *Fantasy, C minor, K.475*

LISZT, *Rhapsody No. 11*

MOZART, *Piano Concerto, A major, K.488*
(*From cadenza by Reinecke*)

4. "SYNCOPATED" PEDAL: MAKING SINGLE CONNECTED NOTES SOUND COMPLETELY CONNECTED

Although the notes are connected with the fingers, they should also be connected with the pedal. This is generally called "syncopated" pedal. It is marked thus:

Put the pedal down *a moment after* the opening note is struck (as indicated previously). Hold the pedal until the next note, and lift it the moment the note is struck (just where the notch in the mark stands) and put it down quickly afterwards. Although the foot never loses contact with the pedal, *we must feel through the sole of the shoe* that during the instant the pedal is up, it is *completely* up. This insures *clean* pedaling; the two sounds are connected without blurring into each other.

BEETHOVEN, *Sonata, Op. 28*

BEETHOVEN, *Sonata, Op. 31, No. 2*

BACH, *C# minor Fugue, Well-Tempered Clavier, Book I*

MOZART, *Fantasy, C minor, K.475*

4

CESAR FRANCK, *Prélude, Aria et Final*

5. CONNECTING CHORDS, BROKEN CHORDS, ARPEGGIOS AND HARMONIES WITH THE PEDAL IN SUSTAINED MUSIC

Change pedal with each change of harmony (always using syncopated pedal).

BEETHOVEN, *"Waldstein" Sonata, Op. 53*

BEETHOVEN, *"Waldstein" Sonata, Op. 53*

BEETHOVEN, *"Moonlight" Sonata, Op. 27, No. 2*

Often, in very delicate music, the soft pedal (una corda) is taken at the same time with the damper pedal. The rules for the damper pedal remain the same.

CHOPIN, *Nocturne, G minor, Op. 37, No. 1*

MOZART, *Sonata, C major, K.545*

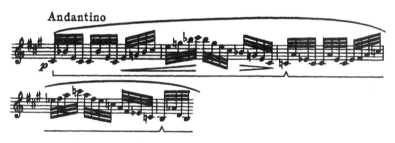

SCHUBERT, *Sonata, A major, Op. Posth.*

6. MELODIES WITH PASSING NOTES IN THE RIGHT HAND, OVER RICH ACCOMPANIMENT IN THE LEFT HAND, ARE PLAYED WITH CONTINUOUS SYNCOPATED PEDAL.

Passing notes in the right hand melody do not blur when the harmony in the lower register of the piano is definitely established, and when the accompaniment is softer than the melody.

6

CHOPIN, *Nocturne, Db major, Op. 27, No. 2*

CHOPIN, *Nocturne, F# minor, Op. 48, No. 2*

SCHUMANN, *"Des Abends," from Fantasiestücke, Op. 12*

MENDELSSOHN, *Song without Words, G major, Op. 62, No. 1*

SINDING, *Serenade*, Op. 33, No. 4

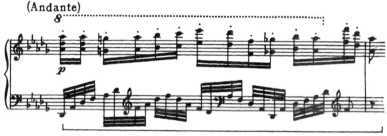

VERDI-LISZT, *Rigoletto Paraphrase*

CH. M. LOEFFLER, *A Pagan Poem*

In pieces where the melody is built on a series of rich, full harmonies—such as the Chopin Etudes Opus 10, No. 1, Opus 25, No. 1, Opus 25, No. 12; Chopin Preludes, Opus 28, No. 1,

8

No. 8, No. 19—the pedal is used continuously throughout the piece, changing it with each harmony by syncopated pedal, but making a *clean change* each time.

Passing notes even in middle voices can be blurred by the pedal, provided the obscurity lasts only a fraction of a second.

BRAHMS, *Intermezzo, Op. 117, No. 2*

7. BLENDING UPPER AND LOWER REGISTERS OF THE PIANO IN COMBINED SOUND

CHOPIN, *Scherzo, B♭ minor, Op. 31*

Later:
(Più mosso)

CHOPIN, *Scherzo, C# minor, Op. 39*

Beginning the arpeggio *piano* after the *forte* bass and gradually increasing the volume of the passage makes a perfect blending of the rich tone-mass. If *all* the notes of these passages were played *loud,* it would sound simply thick, rather than brilliant.

LISZT, *Liebestraum No. 3*

In reverse, this procedure has the unique effect of *diminishing* the tone-mass.

CHOPIN, *Barcarolle, Op. 60*

In some editions of the foregoing examples one finds strange and incomprehensible pedal marks. In these editions the basses and the harmonies above them have separate pedals, destroying the effect of the combined sound. Where these romantic outbursts should sound rich and glamorous they sound dry and academic.

SCHUMANN, *Carnaval (Préambule)*

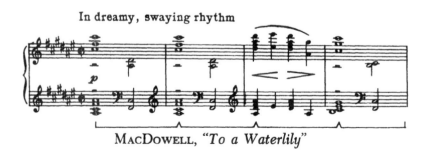

MACDOWELL, *"To a Waterlily"*

Andantino

GEBHARD, *Sunlight through the Trees*

8. ABOUT STACCATO, HALF LEGATO AND LEGATO, WITHOUT PEDAL AND WITH PEDAL

Many people still think that all staccato notes on the piano should be played without pedal, thinking that any two or more notes played in succession with pedal sound legato. People who believe this do not listen well. The modern pianist plays some staccato notes without pedal and some with. Both sound staccato but they are of two different flavors. Play the following slowly on the piano:

1. Play staccato, short, with the fingers and hand, without pedal. You hear a *dry staccato*.

2. Play staccato as before, but hold the pedal through it all. If you listen carefully, it still sounds staccato, but it has a more *liquid* sound. It does not sound legato or half-legato. We call this *liquid staccato*.

3. Play half-legato with the hand and fingers—not short, but not quite connecting the notes, and without pedal. This is a *dry portamento*.

4. Now play it again the same way, but hold the pedal through it all. This is a *liquid portamento*.

5. Now play legato—connect with the fingers, without pedal. This is a *dry legato.*

6. Play legato again, but hold the pedal through it all. You hear a *liquid legato.*

Six different effects are thus available:

1. Dry staccato ....without pedal
2. Liquid staccato.......................with pedal
3. Dry portamento.................without pedal
4. Liquid portamento...................with pedal
5. Dry legato.........................without pedal
6. Liquid legato...........................with pedal

We have found that staccato, portamento (half-legato) and legato can be distinguished from one another when the pedal is down as well as when it is up. In other words, we can produce staccato, portamento and legato, each with two different flavors, *without pedal* when it has a *dry* flavor, and *with pedal* when it has a *liquid* flavor. Thousands of examples can be given from the piano literature where one of these different effects will be appropriately musical and artistic. Examples of applications of each one follow:

Dry staccato, without pedal:

MENDELSSOHN, *Scherzo in E minor*

Liquid staccato, with pedal:

LIADOV, *"Music-Box"*

Dry portamento, without pedal:

(Allegro)

BEETHOVEN, *Sonata, Op. 14, No. 1*

Liquid portamento, with pedal:

espressivo

MOZART, *Piano Concerto, D minor, K.466*

Dry legato, without pedal:

BACH, *Eb minor Fugue (Well-Tempered Clavier, Bk. 1)*

Liquid legato, with pedal:

Andante

p

CHOPIN, *Nocturne, Op. 55, No. 1*

When we consider the variety of expression (aside from rhythmic varieties) we obtain by dynamics (shading from *pp* to *ff*) and occasional use of the soft pedal *(una corda)*—and add to this the six pedal effects just explained (three without pedal, dry—and three with pedal, liquid) we increase our palette of tone-painting a hundred-fold.

9. PEDALING WITH THE PHRASE

Especially in brusque, abrupt phrases fingers and foot may be lifted simultaneously, making for a highly dramatic effect.

Presto con fuoco

CHOPIN, *Scherzo, C♯ minor, Op. 39*

(Allegro risoluto)

BRAHMS, *Rhapsody, Op. 119, No. 4*

LISZT, *Hungarian Fantasy*

SCHUMANN, *Papillons, Op. 2*

PEDALING AGAINST THE PHRASE, especially elegant and graceful phrases.

(Allegretto)

CHOPIN, *Ballade, A♭ major, Op. 47*

SCHUMANN, *Papillons, Op. 2*

PEDALING THROUGH THE PHRASE

BEETHOVEN, *Sonata, Op. 31, No. 3*

BEETHOVEN, *"Emperor" Concerto, Op. 73*

In the last four examples the phrasing can be distinctly heard through the pedal. But if these examples were played without pedal, the music would sound dry and choppy.

10. IN MODERATELY FAST MELODIES THAT CONTAIN VARIOUS TIME-VALUES, LONG NOTES MAY BE PEDALED.

MOZART, *Sonata, F major, K.332*

MOZART, *Sonata, B♭ major, K.333*

11. PEDALING TO ACCENTUATE RHYTHM

By courtesy of Durand & Cie, Paris, copyright owners.
BACH–SAINT-SAENS, *Bourrée in B minor*

CHOPIN, *Mazurka, Op. 6, No. 1*

PEDALING ON DIFFERENT BEATS OF THE MEASURE
This procedure will enhance the lilt and swing of dance-like passages.

CHOPIN, *Mazurka, Op. 7, No. 3*

CHOPIN, *Mazurka, Op. 59, No. 3*

SCHARWENKA, *Polish Dance*

CHOPIN, *Waltz, F major, Op. 34, No. 3*

18

CHOPIN, *Waltz, C# minor, Op. 64, No. 2*

JOHANN STRAUSS, *Waltz, "Wiener Blut"*

MARGARET GEBHARD PETRICK, *Tango*

SHOSTAKOVICH, *Polka, from "L'age d'or," Opus 22*

(Allegro moderato)

LECUONA, *Malagueña*

BARTOK, *Allegro Barbaro*

(Modéré)

DEBUSSY, *Minstrels*

In the traditional dance forms—the gavotte, minuet, mazurka, waltz, etc.—the greater part of the basses are conventional ones. This means: *pedal* on the *first* beat of the measure and hold one or two beats, or a whole bar, according to the musical content of the passage. In the rest of the music, which may feature unusual phrasing, accents, etc., we apply the special pedalings indicated in the foregoing examples.

In pieces full of rapid, even passages in the right hand supported by a rhythmic accompaniment in the left hand (as in some Chopin Etudes) the pedaling should be governed by the left hand's rhythmic content. An example may be found in the *Black Key Etude*, Op. 10, No. 5 (right hand part omitted).

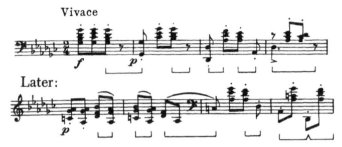

On the above principle we can also pedal the Chopin Etudes, Op. 10, Nos. 4, 7 and 8, and Op. 25, Nos. 6 and 11.

12. PEDALING FOR COLORS—BLURRING NOTES AND HARMONIES IN THE HIGHER REGISTER OF THE PIANO TO PRODUCE THE EFFECT OF CHIMES

CHOPIN, *Concerto, F minor*

Other examples of this effect:
GARDINER, *Noël (last page)*
SAINT-SAENS, *Piano Concerto No. 5 (second movement)*
To produce the effect of a music-box:
LIADOV, *Music-Box (quoted on page 12)*
GOOSSENS, *Music-Box*
SAUER, *Music-Box*

A mystical, ethereal effect is gained by blurring such a phrase as this:

BEETHOVEN, *Sonata, Op. 111 (Second movement)*

COLORS—BLURRING IN THE LOW REGISTER OF THE PIANO

The effect of distant thunder:

BEETHOVEN, *"Waldstein" Sonata, Op. 53*

Blurring may heighten dramatic intensity:

LISZT, *Twelfth Rhapsody*

22

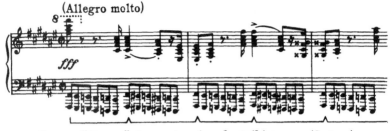

LISZT, *"Orage" from Années de Pélérinage (Suisse)*

COLORS—PEDAL IN IMPRESSIONIST PIANO MUSIC

Impressionism in art means that, whatever "message" is conveyed, it is *suggested* rather than clearly and completely stated. This is true in impressionistic painting (Monet), as well as in impressionistic poetry. The story is not all told; some of it is left to the imagination.

Debussy is the great master of impressionistic piano music, especially in his nature-pieces, such as *Clair de lune (Moonlight) Reflets dans l'eau (Reflections in the water), Jardins sous la pluie (Gardens in the Rain), Le vent dans la plaine (The Wind over the Plain), Cloches à travers les feuilles (Bells through the Leaves), La soirée dans Grenade (Evening in Granada)*. The nature of Debussy's piano style requires that we suggest the picture, not create a photographic reproduction. We play all the notes, but "veil" some of them by blurring the texture with the pedal.

By courtesy of Durand & Cie, Paris, copyright owners.

DEBUSSY, *Reflets dans l'eau*

In *Reflets dans l'eau* we use the soft pedal through the first two pages and last page of the piece, and at the same time use the damper pedal as indicated in the four bars above. The harmonies, played *pp*, blend and blur exquisitely. The little melodic motive  is played *mp*, standing out delicately through the shimmering chordal texture. Throughout the piece we can blur in this way whole measures, or even two or three measures, according to the *broad harmonic basis underlying the blurred tones.* Our musical taste and poetic judgment must dictate the precise application of this. Besides this special variety of pedaling, an exquisite tone and touch are also required to produce the misty atmosphere. Some French composers sometimes attach an indefinite tie to a chord (*laissez vibrer*):

This means to hold the pedal indefinitely. Carrying this idea to the limit, hold the last pedal in Debussy's *La Cathédrale engloutie* and *Reflets dans l'eau* almost until the sound dies out.

(Net et vif)

DEBUSSY, *Jardins sous la pluie*

Blurring these measures suggests heavy, pouring rain.

24

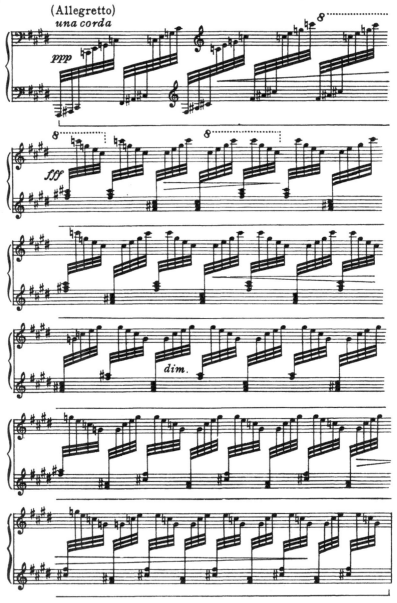

RAVEL, *Jeux d'eau*

Blurring this passage produces a shimmering tone-mass . . .
—a wonderful mixture of the F—sharp major and C major chords.

13. CONNECTING PEDALS

Where it is very difficult to connect notes or chords with the fingers the pedal may be used:

BACH, *Prelude, E♭ minor (Well-Tempered Clavier, Bk. I)*

SCHUMANN, *"Aufschwung," from Fantasiestücke, Op. 12*

If pedaled in this way the chords in the right hand sound connected.

CHOPIN, *Nocturne, Op. 48, No. 1*

14. SHARP, PENETRATING STACCATOS WITH PEDAL

For dramatic effect strike a chord very sharply and allow it to vibrate with the pedal.

Presto con fuoco

CHOPIN, *Scherzo, B minor, Opus 20*

(Molto allegro)

CHOPIN, *Prelude, Op. 28, No. 18*

(Allegro energico)

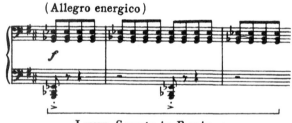

LISZT, *Sonata in B minor*

SHOSTAKOVICH, *Polka, from "L'age d'or," Op. 22*

15. DRY AND LIQUID STACCATOS

Dry; no pedal:

MENDELSSOHN, *Variations sérieuses*

Dry staccato:

Allegro scherzando

By courtesy of Durand & Cie, Paris, copyright owners.
SAINT-SAENS, *Piano Concerto No. 2*

Dry and liquid staccato:

Allegro

SCHUBERT, *Impromptu, Op. 90, No. 2*

Dry and liquid staccato:

Agitato

CHOPIN, *Etude, Op. 25, No. 4*

28

Liquid staccato:

GEBHARD, *Whimsey No. 2*

Liquid staccato:

MENDELSSOHN, *Rondo capriccioso*

Liquid staccato:

SCHUMANN, *Etudes symphoniques*

The chords in the last example are not only "liquid staccato," but they are, so to speak, "liquid connected staccato," e.g., played with syncopated pedal. If they were played with short pedalings (with "air spaces" between them) the piece would sound too brittle, belittling the grandeur of this heroic variation. Strictly observe the rule laid down in (4), *syncopating the pedal even with staccato notes or chords. Put the pedal down immediately after they are struck,* just catching the sound of each chord.

16. BRINGING OUT A MIDDLE VOICE

CHOPIN, *Ballade, Ab major, Op. 47*

Middle voices in difficult and awkward portions are connected by the pedal.

SCHUMANN, *"Chiarina," from Carnaval, Op. 9*

Taking a grace-note-chord with the pedal ("catching it on the wing," so to speak):

BRAHMS, *Intermezzo, Op. 117, No. 2*

This insures against losing any of the complete harmony.

EXTENDING A HARMONY WITH THE PEDAL

CHOPIN, *Impromptu, Op. 36*

17. UNUSUAL EFFECTS

BEETHOVEN, *"Moonlight" Sonata, Op. 27, No. 2*

We hear the big tone-mass until ♪; we then change the pedal, still holding the chord, which we then hear clearly without the underlying tone-mass. A striking effect.

"PHANTOM" CHORDS

Strike this chord silently. After four or five seconds change the pedal and hold the chord.

LISZT, *Etude, "Un Sospiro"*

SCHUMANN, *"Paganini," from Carnaval, Op. 9*

Arnold Schoenberg in his *Klavierstücke*, Op. 11, uses "phantom" notes in this way.

18. CONTRASTS

Effective contrasts are possible through pedaling extended passages in a piece. In one of my lessons with Leschetizky in Vienna, during one of his talks on pedaling, he said, "Beautiful shading combined with artistic use and non-use of the damperpedal is like fine orchestration on the piano."

While studying the score of *Tristan* in my orchestration lessons with Richard Heuberger in Vienna, I enthusiastically exclaimed to him, "Isn't it wonderful the way Wagner uses the French horns!," and he answered, "Yes, but it is just as wonderful when he doesn't use them." A lesson in the law of contrast.

In the C# minor Waltz of Chopin the sixteen bars beginning

can be pedaled in four ways:

(a) pedal through the first beat of each bar up to bar 13.
(b) pedal through the first two beats of each bar up to bar 13.
(c) pedal through each bar up to bar 13 (syncopated).
(d) pedal up to bar 13 in any one of the above ways, and bars 13, 14, 15, 16 without pedal. We can also pedal through each bar, holding the last eighth note of each bar into the next bar, like a middle voice (*à la* Klindworth).

(Tempo giusto)

This whole section of sixteen bars comes six times in this Waltz, like a *ritornello*. It makes a delightful contrast in color to play it *the last time entirely without pedal* and *pp*, with the soft pedal.

The same charming effect can be used in the *Minute Waltz* of Chopin. When the sixteen measure-section beginning with

comes the last time, play it (as above) without damper pedal, *pp* with the soft pedal. This color effect can also be done in any quick piece constructed in sections. In the Chopin Etude in F minor, Op. 25, No. 2, although the greater part of the piece is to be done with varied pedaling and shading, play the initial eight bars at their last appearance (at bar 51) without damper pedal, *pp* with the soft pedal.

19. PEDALING BACH AND HIS CONTEMPORARIES

Most of Bach's keyboard music should be played without pedal in piano performances. His music is, of course, essentially contrapuntal and the individual lines must never be blurred. All the fugues (fast or slow) should be played without pedal, as should all the fast or moderately fast pieces. But expressive slow pieces, such as the Eb minor Prelude from "The Well-Tempered Clavier," Bk. I and some of the Sarabandes must be done with pedal to help make them "sing."

Pedal on the chords, but not on the passages of sixteenths. Pedal also on extensive arpeggio-passages, as in the *Chromatic Fantasy*.

All this applies also to Handel, the sons of Bach, and the German and English clavecinists (Pachelbel, Murchhauser, Kuhnau, Frohberger, John Bull, Byrd, Purcell, etc.). In Couperin we use delicate touches of pedal here and there in the music, sometimes on the first beat of the measure, or on important notes of the melody.

The many quick, scintillating sonatas of Domenico Scarlatti should all be done without pedal. The occasional wistfully pensive pieces should have pedal on the long notes of the melody.

20. HOW TO PEDAL HAYDN, MOZART AND EARLY BEETHOVEN

In the quick movements of Haydn and Mozart the lyric themes should have pedal on the long notes of the melody, as indicated on page 15. Arpeggios and broken chords can be pedaled or not, according to taste. Everything else should be played without pedal.

MOZART, *Sonata in C, K.545*

The slow movements of Haydn and Mozart require pedal, but with discretion. All this applies to the early Beethoven sonatas, *except the slow movements*. Most of the slow movements of Beethoven have a quasi-religious character, even in the early sonatas. They have a depth of feeling found only in certain Preludes and Sarabandes of Bach and some slow Intermezzi of Brahms. Their sustained atmosphere needs much pedal—but *clean* pedaling.

BEETHOVEN, *Sonata, Op. 7*

34

Some purists contend that since the damper pedal had not been invented in the days of Bach, Mozart and Haydn, the keyboard music of these masters should be played without the damper pedal in piano performances, thus imitating the dry tone of the harpsichord. The author feels that if these masters came to life now, they would be delighted to avail themselves of the added resources of the damper pedal, using it with discretion, to be sure.

In some editions the beginning of the last movement of Beethoven's "Waldstein" Sonata, Op. 53, shows some surprising pedal marks by the composer. The tonic and dominant are blurred. The author cannot agree with these indications. The damper pedal was new at that time, and Beethoven experimented with it. (Similar directions are found in the slow movement of his C minor Concerto.)

It is feasible and even appropriate to blur harmonies of the impressionistic school, as in Debussy. But to obscure basic harmonies in the classic school is offensive to the ear.

21. HOW MUCH PEDAL IN MODERN PIANO MUSIC?

Speaking generally, the pedal in modern piano music should be used sparingly. In fact, there are some contemporary piano pieces which should be played entirely without pedal—but on the other hand, there are places where clashing harmonies should be deliberately "melted" together with the pedal.

KHATCHATURIAN, *Toccata*

Modern lyrical themes are pedaled like Haydn or Mozart themes—pedal on the long notes. Many quick passages have a *percussive* character and should be played *staccato* and sometimes *martellato* (hammered), without pedal. The first section of the Scherzo of the Hovhaness Sonata, Opus 2 (the first 66 measures) is played entirely without pedal. The following can also be played entirely without pedal:

KABALEVSKY: *Sonatina, Op. 13*

SHOSTAKOVICH: *Nos. 5 and 15 of the Preludes, Op. 34*

VILLA-LOBOS: *Polichinelle*

Some French composers write the word *sec* (dry) when they require "no pedal," for instance at the end of Debussy's *Minstrels* and *General Lavine*.

There are cases when a piece can be played entirely without pedal, or with touches of pedal here and there, according to the performer's taste.

LEONARD BERNSTEIN, *Anniversary 1948, No. 4*
For Helen Coates

According to the composer's remarks to me, this work "can be played without pedal." Nonetheless, he himself uses little touches, such as: "page 9—bar 9—just a touch of pedal for the crescendo—top of page 10—for the cantabile only—last bar of page 10—just a little pedal; light touches of pedal elsewhere, but always very sparingly."

22. HALF-PEDAL

When a harmony has been sounded over a great range of the keyboard—with chords, broken chords or arpeggios—and we would like to hear the sound die out by degrees, we employ "half pedal." The effect is gained by lifting the pedal only half way up, and using a rapid oscillating motion of the foot.

Little by little the sound "disappears into thin air"—a beautiful effect.

BEETHOVEN, *"Appassionata" Sonata, Op. 57*

Through the gradually vanishing harmony we can still hear:

The Sostenuto Pedal

MOST MODERN GRAND PIANOS HAVE, BESIDES THE DAMPER AND soft pedals, a third pedal, usually called the *sostenuto pedal*. Its function is to allow certain selected tones to continue sounding, leaving the hands free to play elsewhere. The sostenuto pedal—the middle one of the three pedals—is designated *S.P.*, and is usually taken with the left foot. It must be taken shortly after the tone or tones to be prolonged have been struck. Its release is indicated by a star (*). There are hundreds of piano-pieces in which there is no occasion or necessity to use this pedal. But there are compositions where it is extremely useful and even necessary in places where a note or notes must continue to sound through other notes that would otherwise be out of reach.

The idea of one note being static while the rest of the music moves about suggests an organ-point. Therefore, as first illustrations, we quote a number of organ-points from Bach organ works, in piano transcriptions by Tausig, Liszt, Busoni and others.

BACH, *Organ Toccata, D minor*

Strike the bass-octave D, and soon after depress the sostenuto pedal. Hold the bass long enough to insure that the S.P. has securely "anchored" it. Then play the rest of the music as written, with the free hands. Then release foot and hands at the star (*). Further illustrations of the use of the sostenuto pedal may be found in the following examples:

BACH, *Organ Toccata, D minor*

BACH, *Organ Praeludium, A minor*

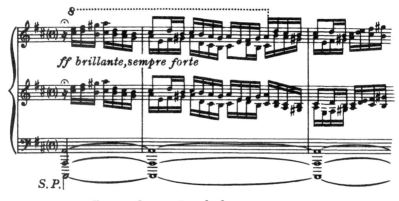

BACH, *Organ Praeludium, D major*

BACH, *Organ Praeludium, D major (continued)* ✽

S.P.

dim.

BACH, *Organ Fugue, C major* ✽

Allegro   Later:

S.P.

SCHUMANN, *Toccata, Op. 7* ✽

LISZT, *Hungarian Rhapsody No. 13*

(Presto con fuoco)

CHOPIN, *Ballade, G minor, Opus 23* *

S.P. hold *until* *

SAINT-SAENS, *Piano Concerto No. 2, Op. 22*

Later:

SAINT-SAENS, *Piano Concerto No. 2, Op. 22 (continued)*

(Allegro)

BRAHMS, *Capriccio, D minor, Op. 116, No. 6*

PROLONGING SINGLE BASS-NOTES

Vivo

GEBHARD, *Whimsey, No. 5*

PROLONGING NOTES IN THE UPPER REGISTER OF THE PIANO

Animato

GEBHARD, *Whimsey No. 7*

Sostenuto Pedal with Damper Pedal

WHEN INSTEAD OF COUNTERPOINT THERE IS A CHORDAL TEXTURE above the organ-point, the damper pedal may be used simultaneously with the sostenuto pedal. Chopin's Prelude, Op. 28, No. 17 (sometimes called the "Bell Prelude") is a case in point. At measure 65 take the low A–flat with the S.P. and hold it until the end, at the same time using the damper-pedal for each phrase, as marked.

CHOPIN, *Prelude, Op 28, No. 17*

The low A–flat—struck 11 times—suggests the sound of a deep, mellow bell.

RACHMANINOFF, *Prelude in C# minor, Op. 3, No. 2*

MacDowell, *"To the Sea" (from Sea-Pieces), Op. 55, No. 1*

S.P. is held to the end of the piece. While moving harmony is connected by the damper pedal the S.P. secures the bass.

Prolonging a chord through a melodic passage:

Chopin, *Nocturne, Op. 48, No. 2*

Chopin, *Fantaisie, Op. 49*

Prolonging a sustained chord through staccato chord:

S.P. *(no damper)*   ✻

BARTOK, *Allegro Barbaro*

Percy Grainger uses the S.P. ingeniously in many of his fine arrangements. In his transcription of Brahms' *Cradle Song* (Op. 49, No. 4), he takes the notes 🎵 silently before beginning the piece, then takes them with the S.P. In the first ten bars, while the damper pedal is changed with each harmonic change, the bass of the droning fifth is assured.

In cases of necessity one may also add the soft pedal. Both it and the soft pedal may be depressed with the left foot. A word of caution against over-use of the sostenuto pedal—pianists sometimes use it where it is not necessary, or even desirable. For instance, in certain cadenzas of Chopin and Liszt which are based on a low fundamental note, they take that note with the sostenuto pedal and use no other pedal. Treated this way these cadenzas sound dry. The use of the damper pedal is at the heart of Chopin's and Liszt's piano style and accordingly most of their cadenzas should be played without S.P., but with the damper pedal and the shadings indicated in ¶7.

The Soft Pedal

THE PURPOSE OF THE SOFT PEDAL IS TO PROVIDE A REDUCED volume of sound. In some upright pianos the pedal merely lets a piece of felt fall across the strings, and in others it simply moves the hammers nearer the strings. In grand pianos the soft pedal—the left of the three pedals—moves the action so that the hammers strike only two of the three strings of each note. Originally, in Beethoven's day, the hammers struck only one string of each note. Therefore the use of this pedal was, and still is, indicated by the Italian words *una corda* (one string), and its release by *tre corde* (three strings).

There are two general purposes for the use of the soft pedal:

(a) To "round out" a diminuendo making it die gradually).

(b) To create a certain tone-color.

Rounding out a diminuendo with the soft pedal should not be done indiscriminately at the end of any long phrase. And it should be used for a finished musical idea, not just a few notes. The soft pedal in good grand pianos not only makes the tone softer, but it gives the tone a fascinating, mysterious quality, somewhat suggesting muted strings. It is very effective for variety of color if employed artistically and with discretion.

For variety of color, a very obvious use is what is called the "echo effect." For instance, when a short phrase is repeated, play the phrase the first time with normal color, *without* the soft pedal, the second time *pp with* the soft pedal, echoing the phrase.

BEETHOVEN, *Sonata, Op. 31, No. 3*

The "echo effect" can be carried out with longer periods. For instance, in the short movements of the suites and partitas of Bach we can play the two sections of each movement first normally without the soft pedal, with appropriate musical phrasing, shading, expression, etc., then repeat this section with the same expression but with the soft pedal.

In sustained music, particularly of the romantic school, we often use the soft pedal together with the damper pedal.

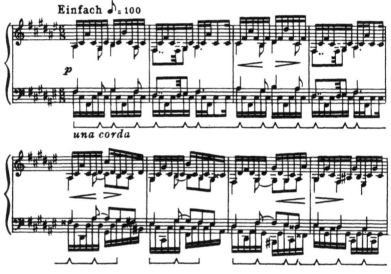

SCHUMANN, *Romance, F# major, Op. 28, No. 2*

Play this opening section the first time with damper pedal and shading, as marked, and the second time the same way, but with the soft pedal added.

THE SOFT PEDAL AS AN AID IN DIMINUENDO

Many slow movements of Beethoven, slow intermezzi of Brahms and nocturnes of Chopin end in a long diminuendo, gradually fading into complete silence at the conclusion. In performance, this is executed with progressively less arm weight; the soft pedal may also be added in the final measures, for a complete fading out.

PIANISSIMO WITH THE SOFT PEDAL ONLY

Certain Chopin etudes admit of various interpretations. Some artists play the Etude in F minor, Op. 25, No. 2 *pp* with the soft pedal only (no damper pedal). Quite delicious. Almost all musettes should be played in this way. The musettes in Bach's Third and Sixth English Suites* are delightful when played throughout with only the soft pedal, *pp*, with no shading. The drone-bass gives the effect of distant bagpipes. This same *pp* effect with the soft pedal is useful for short, delicate nuances, as well as for whole compositions.**

* Gavotte II in the Third English Suite.
** See (18) under Contrasts in Color.

A LONG CRESCENDO AND A LONG DIMINUENDO

Anton Rubinstein's arrangement of Beethoven's *Turkish March* from *The Ruins of Athens* gives the impression of *Janitscharen-Musik* coming from the distance, passing close by, and going away into the distance. One begins *ppp* with the soft pedal (no damper pedal) and increases in strength *very gradually*, lifting the soft pedal when *mp* has been reached, then building up to *fff* with damper pedal; then gradually diminish, taking the soft pedal once again at *mp*, holding it until the end and finishing *ppp*, as at the beginning, with the soft pedal only.

USING BOTH DAMPER AND SOFT PEDALS THROUGHOUT A PIECE

This should be done with the Chopin *Berceuse*. Use the soft pedal throughout the piece, and the damper pedal twice per measure. The delicate rising and falling of the melody and the exquisite passage-work must range only between *pp* and *mp*.

Chopin's Prelude in F# minor, Op. 28, No. 8 can be done with both pedals throughout (damper pedal changing with the harmonies). Violent crescendos and diminuendos may be emphasized with the soft pedal, giving the effect of turbulent inner emotion.

Much of Debussy's piano-music requires the soft pedal, with harmonic blurring with the damper pedal (enlarged upon in (12)).

Movements of mysterious deep feeling which suggest the use of the damper pedal can be greatly enhanced by the addition of the soft pedal:

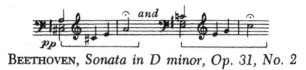

BEETHOVEN, *Sonata in D minor, Op. 31, No. 2*

This motive recalls the mysterious *pp* section for muted strings in the middle of Weber's Overture to *Euryanthe*.

Mystical moments in the last five piano sonatas of Beethoven are evoked with the aid of the soft pedal.

BEETHOVEN, *"Hammerklavier" Sonata, Op. 106*

This movement is full of indications of *una corda* and *tre corde* by the composer.

BEETHOVEN, *Sonata, Op. 110*

BEETHOVEN, *Sonata, Op. 111*

Addenda

PEDAL IN CHAMBER MUSIC

ALL THAT HAS BEEN SAID IN THIS BOOK APPLIES TO THE PIANO SOLO literature. Performing chamber music is another, different art. In music for various instruments with piano (duos, trios, quartets, etc.) the pedal should be used sparingly, in general. Where there is much contrapuntal or rhythmic activity in the other instruments, very little pedal is called for, or none at all. In certain cases, however, where one or a few instruments with a sustained theme are supported by a rich accompaniment in the piano, syncopated pedaling should be used throughout such passages. The piano, however, must remain with the soft pedal added, as in the middle section of the slow movement of the

SCHUMANN, *Piano Quintet*

The soft richness of the piano part adds a warm glow to the theme in the strings.

The same is sometimes true in piano concertos. In the first movement of the Schumann Piano Concerto, the accompaniment of the piano under the theme of the clarinet must have full pedal, but must not cover the clarinet.

SCHUMANN, *Piano Concerto*

In climactic passages where the principal theme is proclaimed by the full orchestra, as at the end of the Second Piano Concerto by Rachmaninoff, the piano part should be played *as loudly as possible, with pedal*—the piano must "fill in" with the orchestra; and there is no danger of its obscuring the theme.

In music for two pianos, besides variety of shading, much variety of tone-color can be obtained through different pedalings. Striking contrasts may be achieved using much pedal on one piano and none on the other. In some light and transparent sections neither piano should be pedaled. In sections where the music is very powerful, rich and heavy, both pianos use much pedal. In some contemporary music for two pianos very unusual color-effects are created by mixing different shadings on the two pianos with the pedals. The effects can be fascinating, bizarre, weird, even terrifying in their dissonances.

What has been said regarding ensemble music holds equally in the special and elusive world of the art song. Though the piano must never overshadow the voice it must participate fully in the evocation of the mood of the text, and no ingredient of piano technic is more important in this task than a sensitive use of the pedals.